Zone Diet

Flavorful Recipes for Lifelong Health

Ava Davis

Table of Contents

Introduction

The **Zone diet**, or **Zone diet**, is a
hyperproteic and low-carb food program
based on the **respect of a precise
proportion between carbohydrates,
proteins and fats consumed**. A diet that
promises to promote weight loss, prevent
diseases and increase mental efficiency, but
which is also highly criticized for the imbalance
between nutrients and the health risks it may
entail.

What is it all about? How does it work? What are its benefits and what are the dangers and contraindications? Find out all about the Zone Diet in our in-depth study.

Zone Diet: what it is

The Zone Diet is a low-carb and high-protein diet that revolves around the **40-30-30 rule: it is** based, that is, on a precise balance between macronutrients, which provides that, both during main meals and snacks, **40% of calories come from carbohydrates, 30% from proteins and 30% from fats.** This proportion is aimed at maintaining a **precise hormonal balance** and **modulation of glycemia** to promote health, weight control and **reduction of inflammation levels** in the body.

History

The Zone Diet was **created by the American biochemist Barry Sears**, an expert in lipids, who through research on eicosanoids, hormones that oversee many functions of the body, has discovered that their correct balance can be decisive for wellness and health. This led him to develop a nutritional strategy able to modulate their production.
But why "zone"? This term, for sportsmen, identifies that state of physical and mental form in which it is possible to improve performance. A condition difficult to achieve, but when it is reached, in jargon "you are in the zone", represents the ideal state for the body.

The first ones on whom Sears tested his dietary method were great athletes: the Zone Diet aims at **extending the benefits of the "zone" for athletes to all those who pay attention to wellness and physical fitness**.

Starting from Sears' studies, some **revisions of the Zone diet** have been elaborated. Thus was born the **Italian Zone, which follows the 40/30/30 criteria of the original American one, but introduces in its nutritional tables also typically Mediterranean foods.**

The Zone Diet for hormonal balance

The Zone Diet assumes that **the body is a complex metabolic device that actively responds to the food it ingests.** In particular, our food choices allow us to modulate **hormones that play a crucial role in well-being and weight.** These include **insulin, glucagon and eicosanoids. The Zone diet, through a precise distribution of nutrients, aims to maintain the levels of these hormones within optimal physiological values.** This results in the reduction of inflammation in the body, the prevention of chronic diseases such as diabetes and heart disease, and weight control.

Insulin and glucagon

Insulin and glucagon are **two endocrine hormones** that primarily function to **control the fluctuating levels of macronutrients, including sugar, in the blood**.
Insulin, also called storage hormone, is produced by the beta cells of the pancreas and regulates the entry of glucose into the cells, which will use it as the main fuel for the body. If the concentration of glucose is adequate, the cells receive the right amount of fuel, but if the concentration is too high, the liver converts excess sugar into fat, which is then stored in the adipose tissue.

Glucagon is the **antagonist** hormone of **insulin** and performs the opposite function: it helps the release of energy stored in the cells. If therefore the secretion of glucagon increases, the organism will be pushed to use the energy, stored in the form of fats, as fuel for its activities.

The Zone diet, through diet, modulates the release of these two hormones, implementing a control of blood sugar.

Eicosanoids

Eicosanoids are an important **category of hormones that regulate many basic functions of the body,** such as **the cardiovascular system, blood clotting, kidney function, immune response, and inflammation**.

These hormones are divided into **two types, "good" and "bad," depending on whether they perform an anti-inflammatory or pro-inflammatory function**.

More specifically, several families of substances (prostaglandins, thromboxanes, leukotrienes) are part of the eicosanoids. **Some, especially those derived from arachidonic acid (omega-6), increase allergic reactions,**

cell proliferation, blood pressure, inflammatory reactions, platelet aggregation, thrombogenesis and vasospasm, produce LDL cholesterol and decrease HDL cholesterol. **Those derived from EPA and DHA (Omega-3), have opposite effects, i.e., anti-inflammatory and antiplatelet**. The balance between the two ensures the proper functioning of the body. As in the case of insulin and glucagon, **the Zone diet aims to modulate through the diet the production of "good" eicosanoids and "bad" eicosanoids** to maintain and promote a state of health and well-being.

Calories don't count

The Zone Diet therefore puts the emphasis on the body's hormonal response to food and different nutrients, in contrast to all the theories that assign calories a central place within a strategy aimed at health and weight loss.

According to the principles of the Zone diet **calories**, which represent the most used tool to establish how much to eat, to choose foods, to compose recipes and meals, **are not the best way to evaluate food.**
An example: **from a caloric point of view, carbohydrates and proteins are equivalent**, because they both provide 4.1 calories per gram. But **the hormonal response they induce is opposite**: carbohydrates stimulate the production of insulin, proteins act on glucagon. According to the principles of the Zone diet, disregarding this aspect can lead to wrong conclusions about the cause of weight gain. This does not mean that in order to lose weight one must eat only proteins, it means however that calories are not the only parameters to be considered in order to set a correct diet.

Zone Diet: the benefits

Here are the main benefits that the Zone diet allows you to obtain. These positive effects are a consequence of the control of glycemia and the reduction or prevention of the inflammatory state of the body.

- **Reduced incidence of chronic diseases** related to the metabolic syndrome, such as cardiovascular disease, type 2 diabetes, obesity, and Alzheimer's disease.
- **Improved cognitive performance**.
- **Increased energy levels and improved physical performance**, because the stabilization of insulin and glucagon levels puts the body in a position to use fat stored in adipose tissue as an energy source.
- **Reduction of hunger attacks**, a consequence of glycemic peaks after meals.
- **Significant weight loss**.

Zone Diet: the rules

There are 4 **basic principles on which the zone diet is based**:

- Follow the **40-30-30 rule in nutrient breakdown: 40% carbohydrate, 30% protein, 30% fat**.
- **Fractionate meals over 24 hours**: it is important that no **more than 4/5 hours** elapse **between a main meal and a snack and more than 3 hours** elapse between **a snack and the next meal** (excluding night time). It is advisable to have breakfast within half an hour after waking up and a snack half an hour before going to sleep.
- **Supplement your diet with Omega 3**.
- Combine diet with **moderate but regular exercise**.

The block system

The cornerstone around which the Zone diet revolves is the block system. The **block** is the **tool that allows the correct combination**

of foods, from the point of view of both quality and quantity.
Each person, depending on age, sex, and the more or less active life they lead, has a **different dietary requirement, which translates into a greater or lesser number of blocks**. The block is therefore the brick that, alone or combined with others, forms **the basis of all meals of the day**. **Each complete block consists of 3 blocks, or mini-blocks, of carbohydrates, protein and fat.**
1 block = 1 miniblock of carbohydrates + 1 miniblock of proteins + 1 miniblock of fats

Both blocks and mini-blocks must adhere to the 40-30-30 ratio of carbohydrates, protein, and fat.

In detail, **each block contains**:

- 1 miniblock of Carbohydrates = 9 g
- one mini-block of Protein = 7 g
- 1 miniblock of Fat =3 g

But how do you know **which foods to bring to the table to make up a block and in what quantities**? The Zone diet provides those who follow it with tables: it is enough to **choose a food for each macronutrient and use the quantity indicated in the table, which corresponds to a mini-block**.

How to start the Zone Diet: step by step guide

The first step to "enter the zone" is to calculate your dietary needs, starting with the protein quota to be consumed every day. This quota will determine the number of mini-blocks of protein, and therefore also of other nutrients, to be provided during the day and divided into various meals.

Here are the **4 steps** to follow:

1 - Calculate Lean Mass

Use this formula:

Lean mass = total weight - % body fat.

You can use an instrument such as a plicometer to measure your fat percentage.

2 - Identify your physical activity index

The physical activity index will serve you, along with the value of lean mass, to calculate the protein quota to be taken.

You can rely on these reference values:

<u>Physical Activity</u>

1.1	Sedentary lifestyle
1.3	No regular physical activity
1.5	Low-intensity physical activity
1.7	Regular physical activity, at least 3 times a week
1.9	Regular physical activity with weights, at least 4 times a week
2.1	Regular physical activity with weights, every day

The different Physical Activity Index values correspond to the grams of protein per kg of lean mass to be consumed, calculated on the basis of the more or less active lifestyle.

3 - Calculate the daily protein quota

Use this formula:

Daily protein quota in g = lean mass in kg x physical activity index.

4 - Calculate the mini-blocks of protein to consume

Based on the protein quota, you will be able to calculate the **number of protein miniblocks to consume daily. Since,** in the Zone diet, the ratio between the miniblocks of the different nutrients is 1:1, every day you should also consume the same number of miniblocks of carbohydrates and fats.

Example: if your protein quota is 100 g, since each miniblock of protein corresponds to 7 grams, every day you will have to consume 100:7 = 14.2 miniblocks of protein (to be

approximated to 14), therefore 14 miniblocks of protein + 14 miniblocks of carbohydrates + 14 miniblocks of fats, for a total of 14 blocks to be distributed in the various meals of the day.

Online **calculators** are available **that, based on your gender, weight, height and measurements, calculate your protein, carbohydrate and fat needs** and **how many blocks to** distribute them in over the course of the day.

Example of subdivision of blocks during the day

Here are a few examples to help you understand how to break down the blocks throughout the day for a man and woman with different dietary needs:

- **11 blocks, for a sedentary woman**: 2 blocks at breakfast, 3 at lunch, 4 at dinner, plus two snacks of one block each;

- **12 blocks for an average active woman**: 2 blocks at breakfast, 4 at lunch, 4 at dinner, plus two snacks of one block each;
- **13 blocks, for a sedentary man**: 3 blocks at breakfast, 4 at lunch and as many at dinner, plus two one-block snacks;
- **16 blocks for an active man**: 3 blocks at breakfast, 5 at lunch and 4 at dinner, a one-block snack mid-morning, a two-block snack mid-afternoon, and a one-block snack after dinner.

How to correctly apply the Zone Diet at the table: foods to eat and to avoid

Protein: lean and from animal and vegetable sources

The fulcrum around which the preparation of a complete and balanced meal revolves is the protein. It is important to **prefer a favorable source (lean proteins) such as white** meat (chicken, turkey), fish, eggs, legumes and derivatives (for example soy derivatives). **Red meat** should instead be consumed in **moderation**.

It's important, even if you don't follow a vegetarian diet, to include vegetable protein sources in at least some meals during the week to reduce your animal protein load.

Few carbohydrates, preferably with a low Glycemic Index

Following the Zone diet requires a **strong attention to the "glycemic response" that each food causes in the blood**, therefore to its consequences on the levels of insulin and glycemia. For this reason, it is fundamental not only to **introduce an adequate quantity of carbohydrates (40%),** but also to **choose those with a low glycemic load, in order to avoid insulin peaks**. The preferred sources of carbohydrates are raw vegetables and ripe fruits.

Consumption of high-GI carbohydrates, such as bread, pasta and pizza, should be very limited.

Plenty of fruits and vegetables

Fruits and vegetables have a fundamental importance in the Zone diet and must be consumed in abundance. In fact, they help to **control the absorption of sugars, avoiding insulin surges caused by carbohydrates**. Fruit also contributes to the **anti-inflammatory action** of the Zone diet thanks to its **richness in polyphenols** with antioxidant effect.

Of course, one should favor those that induce a moderate insulin response, limiting starchy vegetables (such as carrots and beets) and very sugary fruits, such as bananas and figs.

Fats: limit saturated fats, keep an eye on the right omega 3 / omega 6 balance

In the Zone diet it is important to **limit the consumption of saturated fats**, preferring for example white meat to red meat.

The **added fats to be preferred** are those of **vegetable origin such as olive oil, nuts or almonds**. If fatty meats or cheeses are consumed, it is good to reduce the doses of fats or not to use the miniblock of fats because these nutrients are already present in foods together with proteins.

Foods to avoid: Soft drinks; Sucrose; Sausages and fatty meats

Omega 3 and omega 6 fatty acids deserve a separate discussion. These **essential fatty acids** are **precursors of eicosanoids**, therefore the Zone diet, which is aimed at modulating their production through food, suggests a **rebalance between omega 6 fatty acids, precursors of "bad" eicosanoids,** and **omega 3, precursors of "good" eicosanoids**: the ratio between omega 3 and omega 6 should in fact be 1:4, whereas the typical value of the diets of Western industrialized countries is on average 1:10. For this reason, the Zone Diet recommends the **regular consumption of foods rich in omega 3 (such as oily fish, walnuts, flaxseed oil, avocado) or, if necessary, supplementation.**

RECIPES

TURKEY ENCHILADA SOUP A LEAN AND GREEN RECIPE

INGREDIENTS:
- 4 teaspoons Roasted Garlic Oil (or other oil)
- 1.5 lbs ground turkey (or chicken) 97% lean
- 4 C low sodium chicken broth
- 1 T Phoenix Sunrise Seasoning (or low salt taco seasoning)
- 1 T Garlic and Spring Onion Seasoning (or garlic, chives and garlic powder)
- 1 C cilantro leaves
- 1 tsp fresh lime juice
- 6 ounces avocado slices
- 8 Tablespoons sour cream [4 condiments]

DIRECTION
Add oil to a small stock pot or soup pot (with lid) and heat over medium high heat.
Add turkey and saute for 3 minutes, until opaque but not browned.
Break up clumps into small pieces while sauteing.

Sprinkle meat with Phoenix Sunrise and Garlic Seasonings.
Add the chicken broth, stir and cover the pot with a lid. Turn heat to high and bring to a boil, then reduce heat to low to simmer for 20 minutes.
While soup is simmering, chop the cilantro and prep the avocado slices.
When ready to serve, stir cilantro into the soup, divide into 4 bowls and then top with 1.5 ounces of avocado (measure for accuracy) and 2 Tablespoons of sour cr
- Serve

FLAWLESS FLOUNDER A LEAN AND GREEN RECIPE

INGREDIENTS
- 1 3/4 pounds flounder filets (4, 7oz. servings)
- 4 teaspoons Luscious Lemon Oil (or other oil and lemon zest
- 1-2 Tablespoons (1-2 capfuls) Citrus Dill Seasoning (or other blended seasoning of your choice)

DIRECTION
Place oil in a large nonstick frying pan and heat over medium high heat.
Add the fish fillets to the skillet and sprinkle with seasoning.
Cook for 2 minutes then flip the fish over.
Cook an additional 1-2 minutes more until fish is opaque and flaky.
Serve hot.

GARLIC AND CITRUS TURKEY WITH MIXED GREENS

INGREDIENTS
- 4 teaspoons Roasted Garlic Oil (or oil of your choice and fresh chopped garlic)
- 1 C scallion greens, thinly sliced
- 1 3/4 pounds lean ground turkey
- 1 Tablespoon Skinny Scampi Seasoning (or lemon, pepper, garlic, onion, parsley, salt & pepper)
- 8 cups mixed green lettuce
- 1 lemon cut into wedges for garnish

DIRECTION
Place oil in a large skillet and heat over medium high heat.
Add 3/4 C scallions to the skillet and cook for one minute.
Add ground turkey, sprinkle with seasoning and cook for 10-12 minutes until slightly browned and thoroughly cooked. Stir occasionally and break up any large pieces.
Portion 2 cups of greens on to each plate. Top with the turkey mixture and garnish with remaining scallions and fresh lemon slices if desired. A spritz of fresh lemon over the greens and turkey

combination make for a great "dressing" on the salad.

CLOUD EGGS- THE PERFECT BRUNCH!

INGREDIENTS:
- 6 whole eggs, whites and yolks separated
- 2 T grated parmesan cheese
- 1 teaspoon Tuscan Fantasy Seasoning (or just about any other seasoning)
- Nonstick cooking spray

DIRECTION
Preheat oven to 450 degrees. Line a cookie sheet with a silicone baking mat (or parchment paper) and lightly spray with nonstick cooking spray. Separate the egg whites and yolks. I find it easier if you put each yolk in a separate container as they can then be "slipped" into the clouds later on. You can put them in one bowl and then carefully spoon them out one by one in the following step as well. Using an electric mixer, whip the whites into stiff peaks, about 3 minutes.
Gently fold the Parmesan cheese and seasoning into the egg whites using a spatula.
Spoon the egg white mixture on to the prepared baking sheet into 6 mounds.

Using the back side of a large tablespoon, gently indent the centers to form nests for the egg yolks. **If you're making these for a crowd, you can stop here and place the cookie sheets in the fridge for up to one hour. You may, however, need to bake them slightly longer as it will take some time to warm up the cookie sheets. Keep an eye on them so they do not overtake. Bake in the oven until lightly golden brown, about 3 minutes.

Remove the clouds from the oven and gently add one yolk into the center of each puff. Season with salt and pepper to taste, or better yet, give them a pinch of Dash of Desperation Seasoning to make them WOW.

Bake until the yolks are set, about 3 minutes more. Garnish with fresh herbs if desired. Serve hot.

- Serves 2

SLICED STEAK WITH CANADIAN CRUST

INGREDIENTS:
- 2- 10 ounce steaks good for grilling (ask your butcher for suggestions) about 1 1/2" thick
- 1 Tablespoon (1 Capful) Flavor Quake Steak Seasoning (or other dry steak seasoning)

DIRECTION

Trim all visible fat from the steak and pour the capful of seasoning over the meat. Pat the seasoning carefully into the beef so that it sticks. Let the steak rest for 3-5 minutes so the seasonings have a chance to rehydrate. While the steak is resting, turn on your gas grill (or indoor grill, charcoal grill, etc) and heat to 400 degrees F. When hot, place the steak in the center of the grill and cook for 6-8 minutes, seasoning side UP. After 8 minutes, DO NOT FLIP THE STEAK OVER, but rather, using tongs, rotate it 45 degrees. Allow it to cook for an additional 6-8 minutes, or until steak reaches desired temperature as verified by a meat thermometer.

Place the steak on a cutting board and let it rest for 3 minutes. Putting the steak on a super hot grill and cooking on one side only allows a lovely crust to form on the outside while letting the beef cook slowly internally. Letting it rest allows the steak to finish cooking on the inside while also keeping it nice and juicy.

Slice the steak nice and thin, on a diagonal using a very sharp knife (careful!) This allows the crust to stay in place.

Serve piping hot with a lovely side dish! Save the leftovers (if any...) for a salad, sandwich, wrap or to serve with eggs at a future meal. Enjoy!

- Makes 4, 5 ounce servings.

SZECHUAN BBQ CHICKEN WITH SESAME GINGER "RICE"

INGREDIENTS:
- 1 1/4 pounds boneless skinless chicken thighs (or 1 1/2 pounds of boneless, skinless chicken breasts)
- 1 Tablespoon (1 capful) Honey BBQ Seasoning (or 4 Tablespoons sugar-free BBQ Sauce)
- 1 Tablespoon (1 capful) Wok On Seasoning (or other Asian seasoning from your local grocer that is an approved condiment)

Rice:
- 2 cups riced cauliflower
- 1 Tablespoon Toasted Sesame Ginger Seasoning (or fresh grated ginger, spicy red pepper flakes, garlic, salt, pepper and toasted sesame seeds)

DIRECTION
Add chicken to slow cooker. In my case, I forgot to take it out the night before, so I put it in frozen. First, however, I ran some cool water over the

chicken so I could break the thighs into pieces so they fit in the slow cooker.

Sprinkle the seasonings over the chicken.

Cover with the lid and cook for 6-8 hours on low. When ready, remove the cover and using 2 forks, shred the chicken into pieces. Cover with the lid and reduce heat to warm while you're making the cauliflower rice.

To make the rice, simply stir the Toasted Sesame Ginger seasoning into the riced cauliflower and then steam or microwave according to packageDIRECTIONs. Place the chicken over the rice and serve hot.

FORK TENDER BEEF GOULASH WITH PEPPERCORN & SAGE

INGREDIENTS:
- 1 1/4 pounds lean stew beef, visible fat removed and cut into 1 inch chunks
- 2 Cups low sodium beef broth
- 1 Tablespoon Rosemary Versatility Seasoning (or fresh rosemary, sage, poultry seasoning, salt and pepper)
- 1 teaspoon Tricolore Peppercorns left whole

DIRECTION

Place the beef in the slow cooker. In this case, I had it in the freezer and threw it frozen right into the slow cooker.

Pour the broth over the meat

Sprinkle with the seasonings. Do NOT crush the peppercorns or you will wind up with a very spicy and peppery goulash.

Cover and cook on low for 6-8 hours until beef is fully cooked and fork tender.

Serve hot with a delicious green veggie on the side or over cauliflower rice for a complete Lean and Green Meal!

- This makes 4 servings.

SIMPLE SONOMA SKILLET A LEAN AND GREEN RECIPE

INGREDIENTS:
- 4 teaspoons Roasted Garlic Oil (or oil of your choice)
- 1 cup scallions (or onions if allowed on your program)
- 1 cup of red bell pepper, sliced thin
- 1 cup of yellow bell pepper, sliced thin
- 20 ounces thinly sliced chicken or steak (can be cooked leftovers or uncooked)
- 1 Tablespoon (one capful) Phoenix Sunrise Seasoning

DIRECTION
Add the oil to the pan and heat over medium high heat.
Add the scallions/onions and let them cook for 3-5 minutes, until browned on one side.
Add the peppers and stir. Again, let them cook for a good 5-7 minutes until nicely browned. Have patience and just let them cook.... maybe while you're slicing the meat and getting it ready for the next step. The key to getting great color, flavor and char on this dish is a hot pan and patience

Leftover grilled London Broil is a perfect fit for this dish. You can use leftovers of any kind (chicken, pork, etc) with this dish.

When the peppers are soft and cooked, transfer to a dish to keep warm.

Put the pan back over medium high heat and when warm, add the sliced meat. Sprinkle seasoning over the meat and cook for 5-7 minutes (or longer if using raw meat) stirring occasionally.

When the meat is fully cooked, add the peppers back to the pan and stir to incorporate (and warm up the peppers.)

Serve hot as a main dish, or over greens as a salad.

- Makes 4 servings

ITALIAN FRITTATA A LEAN AND GREEN RECIPE

INGREDIENTS:
- 6 large eggs
- 1/4 Cup unsweetened almond milk
- 2 teaspoons Roasted Garlic Oil (or high quality regular oil and fresh garlic)
- 1 Cup baby spinach
- 1 Cup zucchini, sliced in half lengthwise then cut into thin slices
- 1 Tablespoon (one capful) Tuscan Fantasy Seasoning (or natural sea salt, garlic, fresh cracked pepper, parsley, red bell pepper & onion)
- 1 Cup cherry tomatoes, halved

DIRECTION
Preheat oven to 375 degrees F.
Whisk together eggs, almond milk. Set aside.
(Note- for a fluffier frittata, do this in a blender or mix with an immersion blender.)
Place an 8″ oven safe skillet on medium high heat on the stovetop (NO plastic handle- careful!) Add the oil to the pan and heat.

Add the remaining ingredients and cook for 2-4 minutes until greens wilt and zucchini starts to soften.

Pour the eggs in the pan.

Turn the stove off and carefully slide the skillet into the oven (you can put on a cookie sheet if it's easier for you.)

Bake for 25-30 minutes, until the eggs are set.

Remove from the oven and let rest for 10 minutes.

Slice and serve! Great hot or chilled.

- Serves 2

ULTIMATE LEAN AND GREEN BURGER

INGREDIENTS:

- 20 ounces lean ground beef (preferably organic and grass fed)
- 1 1/2 Tablespoons Simply Brilliant Seasoning

DIRECTION

Add seasoning to the ground beef.
Combine thoroughly.
Portion beef into 4 segments.
Flatten in your hands to patties a little less than 1/2" thickness.
Place on an outdoor grill, indoor grill, frying pan or in the broiler.
Cook for 2-4 minutes on each side until desired temperature is reached.
Serve hot!

- Makes 4, 5 ounce patties that are 1 Lean and 1 Condiment each.

TENDER & TANGY BBQ RIBS- A LEAN AND GREEN RECIPE

INGREDIENTS:
- 1/4 C apple cider vinegar
- 1/4 C water
- 2 lbs boneless pork ribs, all visible fat trimmed off & discarded
- 1-2 Tablespoons (1-2 Capfuls) Honey BBQ Seasoning Sugar Free BBQ Sauce – Mesquite Style (or your favorite)

DIRECTION
Pour vinegar and water into the bottom of the slow cooker.
 Arrange the ribs in the slow cooker, preferably in a single layer.
Sprinkle the seasoning generously over the ribs.
Place cover on the slow cooker and cook on low for 6-8 hours, until fork tender.
Lightly brush with BBQ Sauce* and serve with your favorite side dish!
- Makes approximately 7, 5 ounce servings.

RESTAURANT QUALITY BROCCOLI RABE WITH GARLIC

INGREDIENTS:
- 1 bunch fresh broccoli rabe
- 1/2 C chicken stock or broth
- 1 Tablespoon (1 capful) Garlic and Spring Onion Seasoning

DIRECTION
Add the broccoli rabe to a shallow frying pan and sprinkle with seasoning.

Add the liquid and set heat to high.

Let the liquid boil then reduce the heat to medium. Cover with a lid and cook for 5-8 minutes, until the stems are fork tender.

Remove broccoli rabe from the pan using tongs, and let it "hang" over the pan for a minute to allow excess liquid to run off.

Season with salt and pepper if desired and serve hot.

GLAZED GINGER CHICKEN AND GREEN BEANS A LEAN AND GREEN RECIPE

INGREDIENTS
- 1 Tablespoon Toasted Sesame Ginger Seasoning
- 1 1/2 pounds boneless skinless chicken (breasts or thighs)
- nonstick cooking spray
- 1/4 Cup low sodium soy sauce
- 1/2 Cup water
- 4 cups fresh green beans, ends snipped

DIRECTION
Sprinkle the Toasted Sesame Ginger over the chicken & gently pat it to stick. Let it sit for up to 15 minutes to let flavors blend.

Spray a large frying pan with nonstick cooking spray and heat over medium high heat. Note- I love to use cast iron for this as it makes such a great crust on the chicken.

Place the chicken in the frying pan, sesame seed side DOWN & let it cook for 5-7 minutes, until the sides are opaque as in the photo below.

Turn the chicken over and cook for 5-7 additional minutes, until chicken is thoroughly cooked.

Remove the chicken from the pan and set aside.
Pour the water and soy sauce into the pan, scraping
the fond off the bottom (the stuck "stuff"). This will
make a really yummy sauce for the chicken.
Place the pan back over medium-high heat and
bring to a boil. Once boiling, reduce the heat to
medium, add the beans and cook for 5-7 minutes,
until fork tender. Stir them occasionally while
cooking.
When tender, add to plate with the chicken, pour
the sauce over the chicken and beans and serve!
Serve hot as a main dish, or chilled and sliced over
salad.

MELT IN YOUR MOUTH POT ROAST A LEAN AND GREEN RECIPE

INGREDIENTS:
- 2 1/2 lbs lean chuck roast (pot roast) visible fat removed
- 28 oz can diced tomatoes (not crushed, or stewed and nothing flavored)
- 1-2 Tablespoons (1-2 capfuls) Garlic and Spring Onion Seasoning

DIRECTION
Add the beef to the Crock Pot / Slow Cooker or InstaPot
Pour the tomatoes over the beef.
Sprinkle with seasoning.
Cover with the lid and cook on low for 8-10 hours, until fork tender. Basically throw it all in and let it cook all day! Effortless.
- Serves 8

TENDER BEEF STEW WITH ROSEMARY
A LEAN AND GREEN RECIPE

INGREDIENTS:
- 4 teaspoons Roasted Garlic Oil
- 1 C scallions, chopped (whites only)
- 4 cloves fresh garlic
- 2 1/2 pounds lean stew beef (I use pot roast) cut into 1" chunks
- 2 Tablespoon (2 capfuls) Rosemary Versatility Seasoning
- 4 Cups beef stock
- 1/2 Tablespoon Dash of Desperation Seasoning

DIRECTION
Add 1/2 of the Roasted Garlic oil to a large skillet or pot (if cooking the stew on the stovetop and not a slow cooker) and heat over medium high heat.
While the oil is heating, dry the beef off on all sides with a paper towel. Being dry will help it to brown better.
When the oil is sizzling, add 1/2 of the beef and let it cook for 3-4 minutes on two sides until it's nice and brown. Remove the beef and set aside.
Place the pan back on the stove and add the remaining oil. Repeat the process with the other

1/2 of the beef and cook until browned. Remove the
beef and place the pan back on the stove.
The beef should have a nice brown crust, but not be
thoroughly cooked when done with the first stage of
cooking.
Add the scallions and garlic to the pan and saute for
5 minutes on medium heat, until the onions are
translucent. You may also add fresh rosemary (like
I did here) if you should have some on hand. It's
not necessary, however.
When translucent, add the beef stock to the pan and
gently scrape the bottom with a wooden spoon to
release all the browned bits from the bottom. This
is called the fond and it is FULL of flavor.
If you are cooking on the stovetop for the full cycle,
simply add the meat back to the pot, stir to combine
and cover with a tight lid. Turn the heat to low and
simmer for 4 hours until the beef is fork-tender.
If you are cooking in a crock pot or slow cooker, add
all the ingredients to the slow cooker, stir to
combine and cover with the lid. Cook on low for 6-
8 hours or on high for 4 until the beef is fork-tender
This amazing dish is absolutely delicious as-is,
served with a salad or steamed vegetables, or served
with cauliflower rice. Also fabulous with rice, pasta
or crusty bread IF you are on a program allowing
these foods.

- Serves 8

TANGY KALE SALAD- A LEAN AND GREEN RECIPE

INGREDIENTS:
- 1 pound of kale, ribs removed
- 4 teaspoons Luscious Lemon Oil
- 2 Tablespoons (2 caps) Tasty Thai Seasoning
- 1/4 C apple cider vinegar
- 1/4 C dry cranberries, orange segments or apples

DIRECTION
Remove the ribs from the kale and pulse in food processor until shredded. Repeat until all the kale is done.
Add the remaining ingredients.
Toss to coat and serve!
Makes 16 green servings with counts as follows below:

ZUCCHINI PAPPARDELLE WITH SAUSAGE & GARLIC A LEAN AND GREEN RECIPE

INGREDIENTS:

- 1 1/2 lbs lean turkey or chicken sausage, Italian seasoned (your choice of sweet or hot)
- 2 C chopped tomatoes (I used cherry, you can use any variety, or canned- but drain if using canned)
- 1 Tablespoon (1 capful) Garlic and Spring Onion Seasoning
- 4 Cups noodles made from fresh zucchini (about 3 zucchini, 8″ long)
- 4 teaspoons Roasted Garlic Oil
- 1 teaspoon Dash of Desperation Seasoning

DIRECTION

Remove sausage from casing and place in a frying pan over medium high heat.
Saute for 7-10 minutes, breaking up the sausage using a spatula as to make a crumbly consistency. (This becomes easier as it cooks.)

While sausage is cooking, make noodles (see video for instruction) and place them in a large serving bowl.

Add tomatoes and Garlic & Spring Onion Seasoning to the sausage, stir in and cook for an additional 7 minutes, until chicken is opaque and tomatoes have softened to make a slight sauce.

Drizzle Roasted Garlic Oil and Dash of Desperation Seasoning over the noodles. Toss with tongs to coat.

Pour sausage mixture over noodles and then, using tongs, "pull" the noodles up from the bottom of the bowl and toss to incorporate sausage and tomatoes through the noodles.

Sprinkle with a little fresh grated Parmesan (if desired) and let sit for just 3-5 minutes so the zucchini noodles soften. Serve hot.

- Serves 4

SAUTÉED SUMMER VEGETABLES WITH LEMON AND GARLIC (LEAN AND GREEN RECIPE)

INGREDIENTS:

- 4 teaspoons Roasted Garlic Oil (or vegetable oil of your choice)
- 1/2 C red onion, sliced
- 3 C fresh zucchini, cut into 1/2" chunks
- 2 1/2 C cherry or grape tomatoes, cut in half
- 1 T Simply Brilliant Seasoning (or fresh garlic & fresh squeezed lemon to taste)
- fresh basil as garnish, if desired

DIRECTION

In a large frying pan, heat oil over medium heat. Sautéed zucchini and tomatoes Lean and Green Recipe

Add onions and sauté for 5 minutes, stirring continually to keep them from browning. They should be soft and translucent before continuing. Add the zucchini and tomatoes. Sprinkle with seasoning and stir to combine. Cook for 5 minutes,

until zucchini are crisp-tender and tomatoes have just started to collapse, making a sauce.
As a cold salad.

- Serves 4

GARLIC CRUSTED FLANK STEAK WITH ROASTED TOMATO RELISH (LEAN AND GREEN)

INGREDIENTS:
- 3-4 medium sized red ripe tomatoes, cut in half
- 2 lbs flank steak
- 1 T Roasted Garlic Oil *
- 1 T Garlic Gusto Seasoning *
- 1 T Balsamic Mosto Cotto(do not substitute balsamic vinegar- use a glaze instead)
- Dash of Desperation Seasoning (to taste)

DIRECTION
Preheat outdoor grill to 350 degrees.
Place tomatoes on the grill, cut side down. After 10 minutes, flip to cut side up.

Make a paste with the garlic oil and seasonings by combining the two together in a small bowl.
Smear the paste on both sides of the steak.
Place the steak on the grill for 2-3 minutes on each side.
While steak is cooking, remove tomatoes from the grill and chop in a bowl. Drizzle with balsamic mosto cotto and a pinch of Dash of Desperation. Toss to coat.
Remove steak from the grill and slice on an angle, against the grain.
Serve steak with a small dollop of roasted tomato relish.
Enjoy!

SONOMA CHICKEN SOUP WITH AVOCADO & LIME (A LEAN AND GREEN RECIPE)

INGREDIENTS:
- 4 tsp   Roasted Garlic Oil
- 1½ lb   boneless, skinless chicken breasts, sliced into thin, bite-sized strips
- 4 scallions whites minced, greens chopped
- 1 T Phoenix Sunrise Seasoning
- 1 T Garlic & Spring Onion Seasoning
- 8 C chicken broth
- ½ C chopped tomatoes (Roma or grape)
- 1/3 C fresh chopped cilantro
- lime, juiced
- medium avocados, diced*

DIRECTION
Stove Top: In a large pot, heat the oil over medium high heat. Once hot, add the chicken and scallions and sauté for 2 minutes. Add seasonings, broth and tomatoes to the pot & stir. Bring mixture to a boil then reduce heat to medium, cover with a lid and simmer for 15 minutes. While soup is cooking, prepare cilantro, lime and avocado. When allotted

time has passed, Stir in the cilantro and lime juice. To serve, place a small amount of avocado in the bottom of each of 4 soup bowls and ladle soup into the bowl over the avocado. Serve hot. *avocado optional

1 serving of soup without avocado is 1 Lean, ¼ Green, 1 Healthy Fat and 1 Condiment. If using avocado, count as an additional healthy fat.

Slow Cooker: Omit oil. Add first 6 ingredients (after oil) to your slow cooker and cover. Cook on high for 4 hours or on low for 6. Stir in the cilantro and lime juice. To serve, place a small amount of avocado in the bottom of each of 4 soup bowls and ladle soup into the bowl over the avocado. Serve hot. *avocado optional

- 1 serving of soup without avocado is 1 Lean, ¼

SEAFOOD & SCALLIONS CREOLE A LEAN AND GREEN RECIPE

INGREDIENTS:
- 2 T butter (or 4 tsp Roasted Garlic Oil if saturated fat is a concern)
- 2 C chopped scallions, whites and greens
- 2 C green bell pepper, chopped into small pieces (but not so small they're minced- see the photos)
- 2 T Garlic and Spring Onion Seasoning OR Simply Brilliant Seasoning
- 3/4 lb pre-cooked langostinos or crawfish or shrimp or bay scallops* (or even a mixture!)
- 8 T hot sauce, any style as long as it is sugar free

DIRECTION
Melt the butter in a large frying pan, over medium high heat.
Add the scallions and sauté (cook while stirring occasionally) for one to two minutes until the whites are slightly transparent.
Add the green pepper. Sauté for 3 minutes until soft and bright green.

Sprinkle the seasoning over the pepper and saute for one minute more.
Add the seafood and hot sauce. Stir gently to combine.
Heat for just 2-3 minutes until they are hot and serve immediately. *Please note if you are using bay scallops, these do NOT come precooked and will need to cook for 5-7 minutes total so they are thoroughly cooked. You will know when they are done when they have turned 100% opaque and white. If you are using a combination of seafood, add the scallops first and cook for 3-4 minutes before adding the pre-cooked seafood. Pre-cooked seafood need only be heated. Overcooking results in a spongy, rubbery and not-so-great texture. Serve hot and enjoy! Fabulous over cauliflower rice.

SEAFOOD & SCALLIONS CREOLE A LEAN AND GREEN RECIPE

INGREDIENTS:
- 2 T butter (or 4 tsp Roasted Garlic Oil if saturated fat is a concern)
- 2 C chopped scallions, whites and greens
- 2 C green bell pepper, chopped into small pieces (but not so small they're minced- see the photos)
- 2 T Garlic and Spring Onion Seasoning OR Simply Brilliant Seasoning
- 3/4 lb pre-cooked langostinos or crawfish or shrimp or bay scallops* (or even a mixture!)
- 8 T hot sauce, any style as long as it is sugar free

DIRECTION
Melt the butter in a large frying pan, over medium high heat.
Add the scallions and sauté (cook while stirring occasionally) for one to two minutes until the whites are slightly transparent.

Add the green pepper. Sauté for 3 minutes until soft and bright green.
Sprinkle the seasoning over the pepper and saute for one minute more.
Add the seafood and hot sauce. Stir gently to combine.
Heat for just 2-3 minutes until they are hot and serve immediately. *Please note if you are using bay scallops, these do NOT come precooked and will need to cook for 5-7 minutes total so they are thoroughly cooked. You will know when they are done when they have turned 100% opaque and white. If you are using a combination of seafood, add the scallops first and cook for 3-4 minutes before adding the pre-cooked seafood. Pre-cooked seafood need only be heated. Overcooking results in a spongy, rubbery and not-so-great texture. Serve hot and enjoy! Fabulous over cauliflower rice.

CEDAR PLANK SALMON WITH LEMON DILL CRUST AN EZ LEAN AND GREEN OPTAVIA RECIPE

INGREDIENTS:
- 1 1/2 lbs wild caught salmon filet
- 1 T Citrus Dill Seasoning
- 1 tsp Dash of Desperation Seasoning
- 4 tsp Luscious Lemon Oilor Water
- 1 cedar plank & 1-2 cups liquid for soaking (apple juice, water, wine, etc.)

DIRECTION
Soak cedar plank for 2 hours. See tips above.
Preheat outdoor grill to 350 degrees
Place salmon on the center of the plank and tuck the thin (belly) side under.
Make a paste from the Citrus Dill Seasoning, Dash of Desperation seasoning and oil or water
Smear the paste over the fish.
Place in the center of the grill over indirect heat for 10-14 minutes, until desired temperature is reached.
Let rest for 5 minutes, slice and enjoy!

FLAVOR QUAKE STEAK SEASONING

INGREDIENTS:
- 2 lbs boneless, skinless chicken, breasts or thighs
- 1 1/2 Tablespoons (1 & 1/2 capfuls) of Flavor Quake Seasoning (no, not just for steak!)
- 4 tsp Roasted Garlic Oil (OPTIONAL!!! use this (or another oil) ONLY if you are using chicken breast to keep it moist. DO NOT use with thighs if you are following a low fat program.)

DIRECTION
Add chicken and seasoning to a large bowl. Toss to coat. Cover and let sit for 15 minutes, up to 6 hours in the fridge.
When ready to cook, preheat grill to medium high heat (about 325 degrees F)
Place chicken on the grill and cook for 4-6 minutes on each side, depending on thickness. Chicken will be done when internal temperature reaches 165 degrees F.
Remove to a platter, let rest and serve warm with your favorite sides*

PERFECT LEAN AND GREEN COLESLAW RECIPE

INGREDIENTS:
- 1 14oz bag shredded cabbage (about 6 cups) with or without carrots
- 1/4 C apple cider vinegar (the good stuff with the Mother)
- 3/4 C plain Greek yogurt- 2%
- 1 heaping Tablespoon Citrus Dill Seasoning

DIRECTION
Add vinegar, yogurt and Citrus Dill seasoning to a large bowl. Whisk to combine.

Pour shredded cabbage over the mixture and using your hands, tongs or 2 large forks, toss the cabbage into the dressing to combine.

Store in an airtight container for up to 5 days in the fridge. Serve chilled.

* carrots are optional and if used, add a negligible amount of complex carbohydrates. If your mix has carrots, please add one additional condiment to the count.

Yields 6 cups.

Enjoy!!

SWEET & SMOKY PULLED CHICKEN A LEAN AND GREEN RECIPE

INGREDIENTS
- 2 lbs boneless skinless chicken breasts
- 2 T (2 capfuls) Cinnamon Chipotle BBQ Dust (sorry, no substitution available for this one!)

DIRECTION
Place chicken in the bottom of your slow cooker (Crock Pot) and sprinkle with seasoning.
Place the lid on (do NOT remove it until cooking is done. Yes I mean it. Really!) Cook on low heat for 8 hours.
Remove lid. Take 2 forks and shred chicken. Serve hot by itself, or taco style with your choice of wrap and fillings.
- Makes approx 6-6 ounce servings

ORANGE GARLIC CHICKEN WITH ASPARAGUS (LEAN AND GREEN / OPTAVIA RECIPES FRIENDLY)

INGREDIENTS:
- 4 tsp Valencia Orange Oil (or 4 tsp oil and 1 tsp grated orange peel)
- 1 medium onion, diced ***OMIT this ingredient if you are on Optavia / Medifast 5 & 1, or following a very strict low carb plan and use 2 capfuls of seasoning instead as onion is higher in carbohydrates)***
- 1 1/2 lbs boneless skinless chicken breast sliced into thin strips
- 1 T (one capful) Simply Brilliant Lemon Pepper Seasoning ** Use 2 capfuls if leaving the onions out**
- 2 C fresh asparagus, woody stems removed & chopped into 1″ chunks

DIRECTION
Prep asparagus by trimming off the bottom woody parts and cutting into chunks. Note that the thinner the asparagus, the more tender the bottoms are and the less waste you have.
 Chop the onion

 Pour the Valencia Orange Oil into the pan and then heat it up over medium high heat.

  Saute the onion for 2-3 minutes, until slightly browned. Skip this part if omitting the onion and go right to step 5.)

Add the chicken and cook for 2-3 minutes until slightly less pink. Then add the   Simply Brilliant Seasoning for that lemony-pepper pop of additional citrus flavor.

Cook the chicken for an additional 5-7 minutes, until almost all the pink is gone, then add the asparagus.

  Cook for an additional 5 minutes, stirring occasionally, until asparagus is tender and crisp then remove from heat and serve hot.

This recipe is fabulous on its own, over cauliflower rice or even served chilled as a cold salad.

GARLIC BUTTER SHRIMP A LEAN AND GREEN RECIPE

INGREDIENTS:
- 1 3/4 lbs   medium shrimp, peeled and deveined
- 1/4 tsp Dash of Desperation Seasoning
- 1 1/2 T Garlic and Spring Onion Seasoning
- 1/4 C chicken stock
- 2 T butter
- Juice of one lemon (or more to taste)
- Fresh chopped parsley leaves (optional)
- nonstick cooking spray

DIRECTION
Spray a large skillet with nonstick cooking spray and place over medium high heat. Add shrimp and Dash of Desperation. Cook, stirring occasionally until pink, about 2-3 minutes. Pour shrimp into a dish & set aside.
Add the Garlic & Spring Onion to the skillet and cook, until fragrant, about 1 minute. Stir in the chicken stock, and lemon juice. Bring to a boil, reduce heat and simmer until liquid is reduced by half (about a minute or so.) Stir in butter until melted
Stir in shrimp and gently toss to combine.

Serve immediately, garnished with the parsley if you desire.

- Makes 4 meals

CREAMY TUSCAN CHICKEN AND VEGGIES- A LEAN AND GREEN RECIPE

INGREDIENTS:
- 4 tsp Roasted Garlic Oil
- 1 1/2 lbs chicken breast, cut into 1/2″ chunks
- 1 T Garlic and Spring Onion Seasoning
- 1/2 C low sodium chicken broth
- 2 C fresh green beans
- 2 C cherry tomatoes, cut in half
- 8 T low fat cream cheese

DIRECTION
Heat oil in a large frying pan (one that has a lid) over medium high heat. Add chicken and cook for 5 minutes, until slightly browned.

Sprinkle with Garlic & Spring Onion seasoning & cook for 2 minutes more until garlic is toasted.

Deglaze the pan by adding the chicken broth and scraping the brown bits ("fond") off the bottom.

Cut or tear the cream cheese into bits and scatter in the frying pan. Add the veggies.Put the lid on the pan and cook for 3-5 minutes more, until cream cheese is melted & veggies are soft.

Remove the lid and stir the melted cream cheese into the chicken to make a thick sauce.

Serve immediately over cauliflower rice or zucchini noodles.

* You can mix and match the veggies to your taste. Just remember, the more color, the better!

- Serves 4

CREAMY TUSCAN CHICKEN AND VEGGIES- A LEAN AND GREEN RECIPE

INGREDIENTS:
- 4 tsp Roasted Garlic Oil
- 1 1/2 lbs chicken breast, cut into 1/2″ chunks
- 1 T Garlic and Spring Onion Seasoning
- 1/2 C low sodium chicken broth
- 2 C fresh green beans
- 2 C cherry tomatoes, cut in half
- 8 T low fat cream cheese

DIRECTION
Heat oil in a large frying pan (one that has a lid) over medium high heat. Add chicken and cook for 5 minutes, until slightly browned.
Sprinkle with Garlic & Spring Onion seasoning & cook for 2 minutes more until garlic is toasted.
Deglaze the pan by adding the chicken broth and scraping the brown bits ("fond") off the bottom.
Cut or tear the cream cheese into bits and scatter in the frying pan. Add the veggies.Put the lid on the pan and cook for 3-5 minutes more, until cream cheese is melted & veggies are soft.
Remove the lid and stir the melted cream cheese into the chicken to make a thick sauce.

Serve immediately over cauliflower rice or zucchini noodles.
* You can mix and match the veggies to your taste. Just remember, the more color, the better!
- Serves 4

CREAMY TUSCAN CHICKEN AND VEGGIES- A LEAN AND GREEN RECIPE

INGREDIENTS:
- 4 tsp   Roasted Garlic Oil
- 1 1/2 lbs chicken breast, cut into 1/2" chunks
- 1 T Garlic and Spring Onion Seasoning
- 1/2 C low sodium chicken broth
- 2 C fresh green beans*
- 2 C cherry tomatoes, cut in half*
- 8 T   low fat cream cheese

DIRECTION

Heat oil in a large frying pan (one that has a lid) over medium high heat. Add chicken and cook for 5 minutes, until slightly browned.

Sprinkle with Garlic & Spring Onion seasoning & cook for 2 minutes more until garlic is toasted.

Deglaze the pan by adding the chicken broth and scraping the brown bits ("fond") off the bottom.

Cut or tear the cream cheese into bits and scatter in the frying pan. Add the veggies.Put the lid on the pan and cook for 3-5 minutes more, until cream cheese is melted & veggies are soft.

Remove the lid and stir the melted cream cheese into the chicken to make a thick sauce.

Serve immediately over cauliflower rice or zucchini noodles.
You can mix and match the veggies to your taste.
Just remember, the more color, the better!

- Serves 4

CREAMY TUSCAN CHICKEN AND VEGGIES- A LEAN AND GREEN RECIPE

INGREDIENTS:
- 4 tsp Roasted Garlic Oil
- 1 1/2 lbs chicken breast, cut into 1/2″ chunks
- 1 T Garlic and Spring Onion Seasoning
- 1/2 C low sodium chicken broth
- 2 C fresh green beans
- 2 C cherry tomatoes, cut in half
- 8 T low fat cream cheese

DIRECTION
Heat oil in a large frying pan (one that has a lid) over medium high heat. Add chicken and cook for 5 minutes, until slightly browned.
Sprinkle with Garlic & Spring Onion seasoning & cook for 2 minutes more until garlic is toasted.
Deglaze the pan by adding the chicken broth and scraping the brown bits ("fond") off the bottom.
Cut or tear the cream cheese into bits and scatter in the frying pan. Add the veggies.Put the lid on the pan and cook for 3-5 minutes more, until cream cheese is melted & veggies are soft.

Remove the lid and stir the melted cream cheese into the chicken to make a thick sauce.
Serve immediately over cauliflower rice or zucchini noodles.
* You can mix and match the veggies to your taste. Just remember, the more color, the better
   - Serves 4

GARLIC BUTTER SHRIMP A LEAN AND GREEN RECIPE

INGREDIENTS

- 1 3/4 lbs medium shrimp, peeled and deveined
- 1/4 tsp Dash of Desperation Seasoning
- 1 T Garlic and Spring Onion Seasoning
- 1/4 C chicken stock (plain, unflavored)
- 8 tsp butter
- Juice of one lemon (or more to taste)
- nonstick cooking spray

DIRECTION

Spray a large skillet with nonstick cooking spray and place over medium high heat. Add shrimp and Dash of Desperation. Cook, stirring occasionally until pink, about 2-3 minutes. Pour shrimp into a dish & set aside.

Add the Garlic & Spring Onion to the skillet and cook, until fragrant, about 1 minute. Stir in the chicken stock, and lemon juice. Bring to a boil, reduce heat and simmer until liquid is reduced by half (about a minute or so.) Stir in butter until melted

Stir in shrimp and gently toss to combine.

Serve immediately, garnished with the parsley if you desire.

HEARTY VEGGIE FRITTATA- A LEAN AND GREEN RECIPE

INGREDIENTS:
- 6 large eggs
- ¼ C unsweetened almond milk
- 1 t Roasted Garlic Oil
- 1 C fresh spinach, chopped
- 1 C green zucchini, sliced into thin coins
- 1 C portobello mushrooms, sliced
- 1 T Garlic & Spring Onion Seasoning
- 1/2 C cherry tomatoes, halved

DIRECTION
Preheat oven to 375 degrees.

Whisk together eggs and almond milk with a pinch of salt. (For a fluffier frittata, do this in a blender). Set aside.

Heat an 8 inch oven safe skillet on the stove (no plastic on the handle!) Heat over medium high heat and add the Roasted Garlic Oil, coating the pan evenly.

Add spinach, zucchini, mushrooms, Garlic & Spring Onion, and a pinch of salt & pepper (or Dash of Desperation for even more flavor.) Cook for just a minute or so – until the greens wilt and the zucchini starts to soften.

Pour in the eggs.
Add the tomatoes. Turn the stove off and next
carefully slide your pan into the oven.
Bake for 20-30 minutes, or until eggs are just set.
Remove from oven, let cool for 15 minutes (or
more), then slice and serve. Add more salt & pepper
(or Dash of Desperation) if needed.

- Serves 2

PEPPERED PUTTANESCA – A LEAN AND GREEN RECIPE

INGREDIENTS:
- 4 tsp Roasted Garlic Oil
- 1½ lb boneless, skinless chicken breasts, sliced into thin strips
- 1 C diced tomatoes
- 1 tsp Viva Italiano Seasoning
- 1 T Garlic & Spring Onion Seasoning
- 2 C multi colored bell pepper, sliced
- 2 T capers, drained

DIRECTION
In a large frying pan, heat oil until sizzling. Add chicken and sauté for 2 minutes, until chicken is opaque. Reduce heat to medium. Add remaining ingredients to the pan. Cover the pan and cook for 5-7 minutes until peppers are soft and chicken is thoroughly cooked. Serve hot.
- Makes 4 servings

LOW CARB CRANBERRY SAUCE

INGREDIENTS:
- 12 oz bag of frozen cranberries (do not use the dry ones!)
- 1/2 C water
- 1 tsp orange zest
- 1/2 tsp Fall Harvest Seasoning
- 4 packets stevia or 30 drops liquid stevia or other sugar alternative
- 1/2 tsp vanilla
- pinch salt

DIRECTION

Zest the orange.

Add the berries, water, zest and Fall Harvest Seasoning to a medium size saucepan. Stir to combine.

Heat over high until boiling. Reduce heat to simmer for 15-20 minutes until berries burst. Remove from heat and stir in remaining ingredients. You can adjust the amount of stevia if you like the sauce sweeter (add more) or more tart (add less.)

Let cool & serve. Store in an airtight container for up to 3 weeks.

- Serving size is 1/4 cup

CREAMY MASHED FAUXTATOES- A LEAN AND GREEN RECIPE

INGREDIENTS:
- 6 C cauliflower florets
- 2 T light cream cheese (Neufchatel)
- 1 T Garlic Gusto Seasoning
- ½-1 tsp chicken or vegetable broth
- Pinch Dash of Desperation Seasoning

DIRECTION
Chop cauliflower into small pieces, (bite sized).
In a large pot, bring enough water to a rolling boil
to cover the cauliflower. Cook cauliflower 6-8
minutes, until very tender, but not overdone. Drain
cauliflower in a strainer.
With the pot empty, put a clean kitchen towel in the
bottom. Pour the drained cauliflower back into the
pot, on top of the towel & remove all excess water.
Remove the towel, leaving the cauliflower behind.
Add cream cheese, seasonings & 1/2 tsp broth to the
pot.
Using an immersion blender (stick blender) or
hand-held electric mixer, or potato masher, mash
mixture until fluffy. Add more broth if necessary.
Season with a pinch or two of Dash.
Creamy fauxtatoes recipe nutrition information

- Optavia Lean & Green Recipe servings / Medifast recipe servings / Take Shape for Life recipe servings / Lean and Green Recipe servings:
- ¼ of this recipe is 3 green and 2 condiment options

LOW CARB STUFFING- A LEAN AND GREEN RECIPE

INGREDIENTS:
- 14 oz fresh cauliflower, chopped fine
- 4T half and half, OR 4T milk OR 4T chicken broth
- 1 T Rosemary Versatility
- 1 t Dash of Desperation
- 8 Grissini style breadsticks- plain or flavored OR 2 packages Medifast Parmesan Cheese Puffs* OR 1/3C Bob's Red Mill TVP**(Texturized Vegetable Protein)

DIRECTION
Preheat oven to 350 degrees.
If using breadsticks, divide the breadsticks into 2 piles of 4 each. Place in a zipper bag and using a rolling pin or can (or another "tool" of choice) pulverize the sticks into medium-sized crumbs. (The bigger you leave the crumbs, the more texture you will have.) If you're using the parm puffs or the TVP, crush them coarsely as well and divide in 2. Add the remaining ingredients to a large bowl and add one bag of bread stick crumbs (or 1 package of parm puffs or 1/2 of the crushed TVP). Mix well.

Pour cauliflower mixture into an 8 x 8 square baking dish.
Sprinkle with remaining bag of breadcrumbs.
Bake for 30 minutes for slightly crunchy stuffing, 40-45 minutes for softer stuffing.

- Makes 4 portions of stuffing.

GRILLED CHICKEN WITH COOL GARLIC "AIOLI" A LEAN AND GREEN RECIPE

INGREDIENTS

- 2 lbs   boneless skinless chicken (breasts or thighs)
- 1 T Dash of Desperation Seasoning
- 1 C Greek yogurt
- 1 T Garlic and Spring Onion Seasoning
- ½ T Garlic Gusto Seasoning

DIRECTION
Chicken
Preheat outdoor grill to medium high heat (you may also use an indoor (George Foreman style) grill or pan sear the chicken as well.
Sprinkle the Dash of Desperation seasoning over the chicken pieces, tossing to coat evenly.
While waiting for the grill to heat up, prepare the aioli.
Place the chicken on the hot grill and cook for 6-8 minutes on both sides until done. Chicken will be fully cooked when it reaches 180 degrees F.
Plate and serve warm with a dollop of garlic aioli.
Add all ingredients to a small mixing bowl.
Using a spatula, fold the spices into the garlic until combined thoroughly.

Let rest for 10-30 minutes before serving to allow flavors to fully blend. Tender Char Grilled Zucchini- a Lean and Green Recipe

TENDER ZUCCHINI A LEAN AND GREEN RECIPE

INGREDIENTS:
- 1 lb zucchini (keep under 1 1/2" in diameter)
- 4 tsp Roasted Garlic Oil
- 1 T Rockin' Ranch Seasoning

DIRECTION
Preheat outdoor grill to medium-high (300 degrees).
Trim ends off zucchini and cut lengthwise in half. Cut halves into quarters or thirds depending on thickness (lengthwise to make long strips.)
Place zucchini flesh side up on a platter.
Drizzle with oil, sprinkle with seasoning.
Place on grill, skin side DOWN and grill for 5 minutes. Flip zucchini and cook 5 additional minutes. Turn off the grill and let rest for an additional 5 minutes.
Serve hot.
- Zucchini Mix & Match Chart! Try any of these, or mix and match your own. With zucchini as a blank canvas, the flavor palate goes on and on!

HERBED LEMON CHICKEN LEAN AND GREEN RECIPE

INGREDIENTS
- 1 1/2 lbs boneless, skinless chicken breasts (or thighs)
- 4 teaspoons Luscious Lemon Oil (or oil, fresh lemon juice and fresh lemon zest)
- 1 T Dash of Desperation Seasoning
- 2-3 T fresh chopped herbs (parsley, thyme, rosemary, chives, tarragon, etc

DIRECTION
Preheat outdoor grill to medium-high heat (about 350)*
Add all ingredients to a large bowl and toss to coat.
Grill for 7-12 minutes on each side until meat is fully cooked (verify with meat thermometer)
Serve hot or chilled.
- Alternate cooking method: place in a single layer on a cookie sheet or in a roasting dish and bake in the oven at 350 for 20-35 minutes. Verify temperature with meat thermometer to ensure doneness.

WARM ROASTED PEPPER SALAD- A LEAN AND GREEN RECIPE

INGREDIENTS:
- 1 lb bag baby bell peppers, assorted colors
- 6 T feta cheese or light cream cheese (if on program) you can also use goat cheese if off program
- 3 T Balsamic Mosto Cotto*** DO NOT SUBSTITUTE WITH REGULAR BALSAMIC VINEGAR as the results will be disastrous. I promise. Use a balsamic reduction instead.
- pinch all natural sea salt

DIRECTION
Preheat outdoor grill to medium high heat, about 350. Wash the peppers & simply throw them on the grill (or use a grill basket.)
Let them cook for 7 minutes, then flip so they roast evenly & cook for another 7-10 until they slightly char and flatten.
Remove from heat and using two knives, cut the peppers into bite size pieces.
Add cheese & drizzle with the Balsamic Mosto Cotto & a pinch of salt and pepper. Serve warm and gooey! Makes 4-5 servings

SALAD

INGREDIENTS

- 4 C Romaine lettuce cut into bite-sized pieces
- 1 C cherry tomatoes, halved
- 2 9-oz. package Bresaola or Prosciutto
- Pinch Dash of Desperation Seasoning

DIRECTION

Add lettuce and tomatoes to a large serving bowl. Gently place Bresaola on top. Drizzle with 1 tsp vinaigrette and Dash of Desperation Seasoning. Enjoy! Serves 4.

- Serving:¼ of this recipe is 1 lean and 1 1/2 green options.

VINAIGRETTE

INGREDIENTS
- 4 tsp Luscious Lemon Oil
- 4 tsp Balsamic Mosto Cotto
- 3T white wine vinegar
- ½tsp dijon mustard

DIRECTION
Add all ingredients to a large bowl and whisk vigorously to emulsify. Store in an airtight container and refrigerate.

- Serving:2 tsp vinaigrette is 1 healthy fat & 2 condiment

CHAR GRILLED TUSCAN CHICKEN KEBABS A LEAN AND GREEN RECIPE

INGREDIENTS:

- 1½ lb Boneless chicken breasts cut into 1" pieces
- 1 C Red bell pepper cut into 1" pieces
- 1 C Green bell pepper cut into 1" pieces
- 1 C Cherry tomatoes
- 1 C Zucchini cut into ½ inch thick slices
- 2 T Tuscan Fantasy Seasoning
- 4 tsp Roasted Garlic Oil
- 3 T Apple Cider Vinegar

DIRECTION

Add all ingredients to a large zipper bag. Seal the bag and massage the marinade into the meat and veggies. Place in the fridge for one hour up to overnight. When ready to cook, Preheat outdoor grill to medium-high heat.

Thread meat and vegetables onto individual skewers, alternating them for best cooking results. Grill for 5-7 minutes on each side, until desired temperature is reached. Use a meat thermometer for best results.

- You may mix and match the vegetables to meet your preferences. In order to make 2 green servings, however, the total amount of veggies used needs to be 4 Cups. Please consult the Lean Options chart for details.

CRUNCHY CAULIFLOWER SALAD A LEAN AND GREEN RECIPE

INGREDIENTS

- 4 Cups cauliflower florets
- 1 Tablespoon (one capful) Tuscan Fantasy Seasoning
- 1/4 Cup apple cider vinegar

DIRECTION

Add all ingredients to a mixing bowl and toss to combine.

Let rest for 30 minutes, up to overnight to allow flavors to combine.

Store in the refrigerator in a covered bowl for up to one week.

GARLIC CRUSTED BBQ BABY BACK RIBS A LEAN AND GREEN RECIPE

INGREDIENTS:
Baby Back Ribs Nutrition
- 1 1/2 lbs baby back ribs, excess fat trimmed & removed
- 1 T   Alderwood Smoked Sea Salt
- 1 T   Garlic Gusto Seasoning

DIRECTION
Sprinkle Salt and Gusto over ribs and spread to evenly coat. Wrap ribs in plastic wrap and place in the fridge for one hour to overnight (the longer, the better!)
When ready to cook, preheat outdoor grill to high heat.
Place ribs on lower rack, cover with bbq grill lid and cook for 5 minutes.
Transfer ribs to the upper rack and cook for an additional 5 minutes. If no upper rack is available, reduce heat to medium.
Flip the rack to the other side and cook for an additional 5-10 minutes, depending on the thickness of the ribs. Test with a meat thermometer to ensure they are done to your likeness.
 Remove ribs from the grill, slice and serve!

CRISP SUMMER CUCUMBER SALAD- A LEAN AND GREEN RECIPE

INGREDIENTS:
- 4 C sliced cucumbers (peels on or off- your choice)
- 2 T apple cider vinegar
- 1/4 C sliced white onion
- 2 tsp Dash of Desperation Seasoning

DIRECTION
Toss all ingredients together in a medium sized bowl. Let sit for 15 minutes to allow the vinegar to mellow the onion and flavors to meld. Serve chilled.

ZUCCHINI & MUSHROOM PARMESAN DUSTED LINGUINI

INGREDIENTS
- Drizzle 1 teaspoon of Roasted Garlic Oil,
- 1 teaspoon of Balsamic Mosto Cotto and 1/4 teaspoon of Dash of Desperation Seasoning over 1 Cup of raw zucchini noodles,
- 1/2 Cup of sliced portobello mushrooms (you can use marinated mushrooms too- just NOT the ones in oil!) and
- 1 Tablespoon of parmesan cheese

DIRECTION
 Toss together and serve for a Lean and Green recipe you'll love. 3 greens, one healthy fat and 2 condiments are all it takes. Feel free to add some cooked shrimp, chicken or beef for a complete meal!

COOL KALE & BOK CHOY SALAD WITH CREAMY RANCH DRESSING LEAN AND GREEN RECIPE

INGREDIENTS:
Salad:
- 3-4 Cups baby bok chop, washed and shredded
- 3-4 Cups kale greens, washed and shredded
- Dressing:
- 4 T light sour cream or low fat plain yogurt
- 1/2 C unsweetened almond milk
- 1 T Rockin' Ranch Seasoning

DIRECTION
Place greens in a large bowl.
In a smaller bowl or shaker container, place all the ingredients for dressing.
Whisk or shake to combine.
Let sit for 10 minutes to allow flavors to develop before serving.
Pour desired amount of dressing over the salad.
Toss to coat & serve!
- Serve with Foolproof Salmon for a complete lean and green meal!

Cooking Basics Checklist

Prepare
- ☐ Read the recipe, do any preheating
- ☐ Get all the ingredients and cooking gear out
- ☐ Prepare all ingredients per the instructions

Work safely
- ☐ Position pot/pan handles to prevent accidents
- ☐ Place a shelf liner or damp kitchen towel under cutting boards to prevent slipping
- ☐ Wash any items immediately after touching raw meat to prevent cross-contamination

Work clean
- ☐ Keep a kitchen towel close to wipe down
- ☐ Wipe cutting boards as you go
- ☐ Keep trashcan or another disposal nearby

Learn basic prep and cooking skills
- ☐ Chop an onion
- ☐ Hard- or soft-boil an egg
- ☐ Poach an egg
- ☐ Cook pasta and rice
- ☐ Melt chocolate
- ☐ Make a scrambled egg or an omelet
- ☐ Bake a potato
- ☐ Stuff and roast a chicken (or turkey)
- ☐ Make gravy
- ☐ Make stock
- ☐ Separate an egg
- ☐ Knead dough
- ☐ Crush and chop garlic
- ☐ Prepare peppers
- ☐ Brown meat
- ☐ Cook a perfect steak
- ☐ Make salad dressing
- ☐ Make batter
- ☐ Rub flour and butter
- ☐ Line a cake tin
- ☐ Make tomato sauce
- ☐ Pit an avocado
- ☐ Whip cream
- ☐ Segment an orange

Master key cooking methods
- ☐ Braising
- ☐ Roasting
- ☐ Boiling
- ☐ Baking
- ☐ Browning
- ☐ Searing
- ☐ Grilling
- ☐ Frying
- ☐ Basting
- ☐ Broiling

Zone Diet

Cooking Basics Checklist

Prepare
- ☐ Read the recipe, do any preheating
- ☐ Get all the ingredients and cooking gear out
- ☐ Prepare all ingredients per the instructions

Work safely
- ☐ Position pot/pan handles to prevent accidents
- ☐ Place a shelf liner or damp kitchen towel under cutting boards to prevent slipping
- ☐ Wash any items immediately after touching raw meat to prevent cross-contamination

Work clean
- ☐ Keep a kitchen towel close to wipe down
- ☐ Wipe cutting boards as you go
- ☐ Keep trashcan or another disposal nearby

Learn basic prep and cooking skills
- ☐ Chop an onion
- ☐ Hard- or soft-boil an egg
- ☐ Poach an egg
- ☐ Cook pasta and rice
- ☐ Melt chocolate
- ☐ Make a scrambled egg or an omelet
- ☐ Bake a potato
- ☐ Stuff and roast a chicken (or turkey)
- ☐ Make gravy
- ☐ Make stock
- ☐ Separate an egg
- ☐ Knead dough
- ☐ Crush and chop garlic
- ☐ Prepare peppers
- ☐ Brown meat
- ☐ Cook a perfect steak
- ☐ Make salad dressing
- ☐ Make batter
- ☐ Rub flour and butter
- ☐ Line a cake tin
- ☐ Make tomato sauce
- ☐ Pit an avocado
- ☐ Whip cream
- ☐ Segment an orange

Master key cooking methods
- ☐ Braising
- ☐ Roasting
- ☐ Boiling
- ☐ Baking
- ☐ Browning
- ☐ Searing
- ☐ Grilling
- ☐ Frying
- ☐ Basting
- ☐ Broiling

Cooking Basics Checklist

Prepare

- ☐ Read the recipe, do any preheating
- ☐ Get all the ingredients and cooking gear out
- ☐ Prepare all ingredients per the instructions

Work safely

- ☐ Position pot/pan handles to prevent accidents
- ☐ Place a shelf liner or damp kitchen towel under cutting boards to prevent slipping
- ☐ Wash any items immediately after touching raw meat to prevent cross-contamination

Work clean

- ☐ Keep a kitchen towel close to wipe down
- ☐ Wipe cutting boards as you go
- ☐ Keep trashcan or another disposal nearby

Learn basic prep and cooking skills

- ☐ Chop an onion
- ☐ Hard- or soft-boil an egg
- ☐ Poach an egg
- ☐ Cook pasta and rice
- ☐ Melt chocolate
- ☐ Make a scrambled egg or an omelet
- ☐ Bake a potato
- ☐ Stuff and roast a chicken (or turkey)
- ☐ Make gravy
- ☐ Make stock
- ☐ Separate an egg
- ☐ Knead dough
- ☐ Crush and chop garlic
- ☐ Prepare peppers
- ☐ Brown meat
- ☐ Cook a perfect steak
- ☐ Make salad dressing
- ☐ Make batter
- ☐ Rub flour and butter
- ☐ Line a cake tin
- ☐ Make tomato sauce
- ☐ Pit an avocado
- ☐ Whip cream
- ☐ Segment an orange

Master key cooking methods

- ☐ Braising
- ☐ Roasting
- ☐ Boiling
- ☐ Baking
- ☐ Browning
- ☐ Searing
- ☐ Grilling
- ☐ Frying
- ☐ Basting
- ☐ Broiling

Cooking Basics Checklist

Prepare

- [ ] Read the recipe, do any preheating
- [ ] Get all the ingredients and cooking gear out
- [ ] Prepare all ingredients per the instructions

Work safely

- [ ] Position pot/pan handles to prevent accidents
- [ ] Place a shelf liner or damp kitchen towel under cutting boards to prevent slipping
- [ ] Wash any items immediately after touching raw meat to prevent cross-contamination

Work clean

- [ ] Keep a kitchen towel close to wipe down
- [ ] Wipe cutting boards as you go
- [ ] Keep trashcan or another disposal nearby

Learn basic prep and cooking skills

- [ ] Chop an onion
- [ ] Hard- or soft-boil an egg
- [ ] Poach an egg
- [ ] Cook pasta and rice
- [ ] Melt chocolate
- [ ] Make a scrambled egg or an omelet
- [ ] Bake a potato
- [ ] Stuff and roast a chicken (or turkey)
- [ ] Make gravy
- [ ] Make stock
- [ ] Separate an egg
- [ ] Knead dough
- [ ] Crush and chop garlic
- [ ] Prepare peppers
- [ ] Brown meat
- [ ] Cook a perfect steak
- [ ] Make salad dressing
- [ ] Make batter
- [ ] Rub flour and butter
- [ ] Line a cake tin
- [ ] Make tomato sauce
- [ ] Pit an avocado
- [ ] Whip cream
- [ ] Segment an orange

Master key cooking methods

- [ ] Braising
- [ ] Roasting
- [ ] Boiling
- [ ] Baking
- [ ] Browning
- [ ] Searing
- [ ] Grilling
- [ ] Frying
- [ ] Basting
- [ ] Broiling

Cooking Basics Checklist

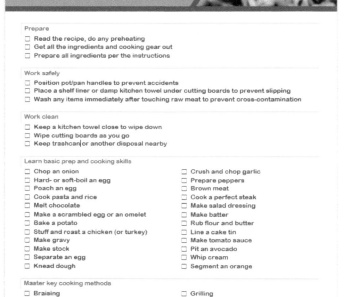

Prepare
- ☐ Read the recipe, do any preheating
- ☐ Get all the ingredients and cooking gear out
- ☐ Prepare all ingredients per the instructions

Work safely
- ☐ Position pot/pan handles to prevent accidents
- ☐ Place a shelf liner or damp kitchen towel under cutting boards to prevent slipping
- ☐ Wash any items immediately after touching raw meat to prevent cross-contamination

Work clean
- ☐ Keep a kitchen towel close to wipe down
- ☐ Wipe cutting boards as you go
- ☐ Keep trashcan or another disposal nearby

Learn basic prep and cooking skills
- ☐ Chop an onion
- ☐ Hard- or soft-boil an egg
- ☐ Poach an egg
- ☐ Cook pasta and rice
- ☐ Melt chocolate
- ☐ Make a scrambled egg or an omelet
- ☐ Bake a potato
- ☐ Stuff and roast a chicken (or turkey)
- ☐ Make gravy
- ☐ Make stock
- ☐ Separate an egg
- ☐ Knead dough
- ☐ Crush and chop garlic
- ☐ Prepare peppers
- ☐ Brown meat
- ☐ Cook a perfect steak
- ☐ Make salad dressing
- ☐ Make batter
- ☐ Rub flour and butter
- ☐ Line a cake tin
- ☐ Make tomato sauce
- ☐ Pit an avocado
- ☐ Whip cream
- ☐ Segment an orange

Master key cooking methods
- ☐ Braising
- ☐ Roasting
- ☐ Boiling
- ☐ Baking
- ☐ Browning
- ☐ Searing
- ☐ Grilling
- ☐ Frying
- ☐ Basting
- ☐ Broiling

Cooking Basics Checklist

Prepare
- [ ] Read the recipe, do any preheating
- [ ] Get all the ingredients and cooking gear out
- [ ] Prepare all ingredients per the instructions

Work safely
- [ ] Position pot/pan handles to prevent accidents
- [ ] Place a shelf liner or damp kitchen towel under cutting boards to prevent slipping
- [ ] Wash any items immediately after touching raw meat to prevent cross-contamination

Work clean
- [ ] Keep a kitchen towel close to wipe down
- [ ] Wipe cutting boards as you go
- [ ] Keep trashcan or another disposal nearby

Learn basic prep and cooking skills
- [ ] Chop an onion
- [ ] Hard- or soft-boil an egg
- [ ] Poach an egg
- [ ] Cook pasta and rice
- [ ] Melt chocolate
- [ ] Make a scrambled egg or an omelet
- [ ] Bake a potato
- [ ] Stuff and roast a chicken (or turkey)
- [ ] Make gravy
- [ ] Make stock
- [ ] Separate an egg
- [ ] Knead dough
- [ ] Crush and chop garlic
- [ ] Prepare peppers
- [ ] Brown meat
- [ ] Cook a perfect steak
- [ ] Make salad dressing
- [ ] Make batter
- [ ] Rub flour and butter
- [ ] Line a cake tin
- [ ] Make tomato sauce
- [ ] Pit an avocado
- [ ] Whip cream
- [ ] Segment an orange

Master key cooking methods
- [ ] Braising
- [ ] Roasting
- [ ] Boiling
- [ ] Baking
- [ ] Browning
- [ ] Searing
- [ ] Grilling
- [ ] Frying
- [ ] Basting
- [ ] Broiling

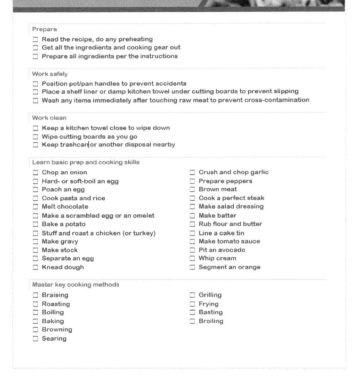

Cooking Basics Checklist

Prepare
- ☐ Read the recipe, do any preheating
- ☐ Get all the ingredients and cooking gear out
- ☐ Prepare all ingredients per the instructions

Work safely
- ☐ Position pot/pan handles to prevent accidents
- ☐ Place a shelf liner or damp kitchen towel under cutting boards to prevent slipping
- ☐ Wash any items immediately after touching raw meat to prevent cross-contamination

Work clean
- ☐ Keep a kitchen towel close to wipe down
- ☐ Wipe cutting boards as you go
- ☐ Keep trashcan or another disposal nearby

Learn basic prep and cooking skills
- ☐ Chop an onion
- ☐ Hard- or soft-boil an egg
- ☐ Poach an egg
- ☐ Cook pasta and rice
- ☐ Melt chocolate
- ☐ Make a scrambled egg or an omelet
- ☐ Bake a potato
- ☐ Stuff and roast a chicken (or turkey)
- ☐ Make gravy
- ☐ Make stock
- ☐ Separate an egg
- ☐ Knead dough
- ☐ Crush and chop garlic
- ☐ Prepare peppers
- ☐ Brown meat
- ☐ Cook a perfect steak
- ☐ Make salad dressing
- ☐ Make batter
- ☐ Rub flour and butter
- ☐ Line a cake tin
- ☐ Make tomato sauce
- ☐ Pit an avocado
- ☐ Whip cream
- ☐ Segment an orange

Master key cooking methods
- ☐ Braising
- ☐ Roasting
- ☐ Boiling
- ☐ Baking
- ☐ Browning
- ☐ Searing
- ☐ Grilling
- ☐ Frying
- ☐ Basting
- ☐ Broiling

Zone Diet

Cooking Basics Checklist

Prepare
- [ ] Read the recipe, do any preheating
- [ ] Get all the ingredients and cooking gear out
- [ ] Prepare all ingredients per the instructions

Work safely
- [ ] Position pot/pan handles to prevent accidents
- [ ] Place a shelf liner or damp kitchen towel under cutting boards to prevent slipping
- [ ] Wash any items immediately after touching raw meat to prevent cross-contamination

Work clean
- [ ] Keep a kitchen towel close to wipe down
- [ ] Wipe cutting boards as you go
- [ ] Keep trashcan or another disposal nearby

Learn basic prep and cooking skills
- [ ] Chop an onion
- [ ] Hard- or soft-boil an egg
- [ ] Poach an egg
- [ ] Cook pasta and rice
- [ ] Melt chocolate
- [ ] Make a scrambled egg or an omelet
- [ ] Bake a potato
- [ ] Stuff and roast a chicken (or turkey)
- [ ] Make gravy
- [ ] Make stock
- [ ] Separate an egg
- [ ] Knead dough
- [ ] Crush and chop garlic
- [ ] Prepare peppers
- [ ] Brown meat
- [ ] Cook a perfect steak
- [ ] Make salad dressing
- [ ] Make batter
- [ ] Rub flour and butter
- [ ] Line a cake tin
- [ ] Make tomato sauce
- [ ] Pit an avocado
- [ ] Whip cream
- [ ] Segment an orange

Master key cooking methods
- [ ] Braising
- [ ] Roasting
- [ ] Boiling
- [ ] Baking
- [ ] Browning
- [ ] Searing
- [ ] Grilling
- [ ] Frying
- [ ] Basting
- [ ] Broiling

Cooking Basics Checklist

Prepare
- ☐ Read the recipe, do any preheating
- ☐ Get all the ingredients and cooking gear out
- ☐ Prepare all ingredients per the instructions

Work safely
- ☐ Position pot/pan handles to prevent accidents
- ☐ Place a shelf liner or damp kitchen towel under cutting boards to prevent slipping
- ☐ Wash any items immediately after touching raw meat to prevent cross-contamination

Work clean
- ☐ Keep a kitchen towel close to wipe down
- ☐ Wipe cutting boards as you go
- ☐ Keep trashcan or another disposal nearby

Learn basic prep and cooking skills
- ☐ Chop an onion
- ☐ Hard- or soft-boil an egg
- ☐ Poach an egg
- ☐ Cook pasta and rice
- ☐ Melt chocolate
- ☐ Make a scrambled egg or an omelet
- ☐ Bake a potato
- ☐ Stuff and roast a chicken (or turkey)
- ☐ Make gravy
- ☐ Make stock
- ☐ Separate an egg
- ☐ Knead dough
- ☐ Crush and chop garlic
- ☐ Prepare peppers
- ☐ Brown meat
- ☐ Cook a perfect steak
- ☐ Make salad dressing
- ☐ Make batter
- ☐ Rub flour and butter
- ☐ Line a cake tin
- ☐ Make tomato sauce
- ☐ Pit an avocado
- ☐ Whip cream
- ☐ Segment an orange

Master key cooking methods
- ☐ Braising
- ☐ Roasting
- ☐ Boiling
- ☐ Baking
- ☐ Browning
- ☐ Searing
- ☐ Grilling
- ☐ Frying
- ☐ Basting
- ☐ Broiling

CPSIA information can be obtained
at www.ICGtesting.com
Printed in the USA
BVHW012329150321
602550BV00005B/585